For

Becky Thatcher

IN THE HOME OF
TOM SAWYER'S BOYHOOD SWEETHEART
209-211 Hill
Hannibal, Missouri
63401

BOOK SHOP

MY BOOK

MARK TWAIN
WIT AND
WISECRACKS

Selected by Doris Benardete
Illustrated by Henry R. Martin

———————

PETER PAUPER PRESS, INC.
WHITE PLAINS • NEW YORK

*The Sayings in this
book are taken from the
various works of Mark
Twain and are reprinted
by permission of Harper
& Brothers.*

Copyright © 1961
Peter Pauper Press, Inc.
202 Mamaroneck Avenue
White Plains, NY 10601
ISBN 0-88088-546-7
Printed in China
7   6

MARK TWAIN

WIT AND
WISECRACKS

Adam was but human — this explains it all. He did not want the apple for the apple's sake, he wanted it only because it was forbidden. The mistake was in not forbidding the serpent; then he would have eaten the serpent.

Do not undervalue the headache. While it is at its sharpest it seems a bad investment; but when relief begins, the unexpired remainder is worth $4 a minute.

I believe that our Heavenly Father invented man because he was disappointed in the monkey.

History is better than prophecy. In fact history *is* prophecy. And history says that whenever a weak and ignorant people possess a thing which a strong and enlightened people want, it must be yielded up peaceably.

There are many humorous things in the world; among them, the white man's notion that he is less savage than the other savages.

I was seldom able to see an opportunity until it had ceased to be one.

I never could tell a lie that anybody would doubt, nor a truth that anybody would believe.

Give an Irishman lager for a month, and he's a dead man. An Irishman is lined with copper, and the beer corrodes it. But whisky polishes the copper and is the saving of him.

Why the Government does not think it well and polite that our diplomats should be able to have . . . credit abroad is one of those mysterious inconsistencies which have been puzzling me ever since I stopped trying to understand baseball and took up statesmanship as a pastime.

The way it is now, the asylums can hold the same people, but if we tried to shut up the insane we should run out of building materials.

Adam and Eve had many advantages, but the principal one was that they escaped teething.

Emotions are among the toughest things in the world to manufacture out of whole cloth: it is easier to manufacture seven facts than one emotion.

The difference between the right word and the almost right word is the difference between lightning and the lightning bug.

I have long ago lost my belief in immortality — also my interest in it.

Loyalty to petrified opinion never yet broke a chain or freed a human soul.

The coyote of the deserts beyond the Rocky Mountains has a peculiarly hard time of it, owing to the fact that his relations, the Indians, are just as apt to be the first to detect a seductive scent on the desert breeze, and follow the fragrance to the late ox it emanated from, as he is himself; and when this occurs he has to content himself with sitting off at a little distance watching those people strip off and dig out everything edible, and walk off with it.

In order to make a man or a boy covet a thing, it is only necessary to make the thing difficult to attain.

Has *any* boyhood dream ever been fulfilled? I must doubt it. Look at Brander Matthews. He wanted to be a cowboy. What is he today? Nothing but a professor in a university. Will he ever be a cowboy? It is hardly conceivable.

By trying, we can easily learn to endure adversity. Another man's, I mean.

When angry, count four; when very angry, swear.

It is the fashion in New England to give Indian names to the public houses, not that the late lamented savage knew how to keep a hotel, but that his warlike name may impress the traveler who humbly craves shelter there, and make him grateful to the noble and gentlemanly clerk if he is allowed to depart with his scalp safe.

Whoever has lived long enough to find out what life is knows how deep a debt of gratitude we owe to Adam, the first great benefactor of our race. He brought death into the world.

How solemn and beautiful is the thought that the earliest pioneer of civilization, the van-leader of civilization, is never the steamboat, never the railroad, never the newspaper, never the Sabbath-school teacher, never the missionary — but always whisky!

Classic: A book which people praise and don't read.

There are people who can do all fine and heroic things but one: keep from telling their happiness to the unhappy.

His ignorance covered the whole earth like a blanket and there was hardly a hole in it anywhere.

Eternal Rest sounds comforting in the pulpit. . . . Well, you try it once, and see how heavy time will hang on your hands.

A genius is not very likely to discover himself; neither is he very likely to be discovered by his intimates; in fact I think I may put it in stronger words and say it is impossible that a genius — at least a literary genius — can ever be discovered by his intimates; they are so close to him that he is out of focus to them and they can't get at his proportions; they cannot perceive that there is any considerable difference between his bulk and their own.

Happiness ain't a *thing in itself* — it's only a *contrast* with something that ain't pleasant.

Man is the only animal that blushes. Or needs to.

Switzerland is simply a large humpy, solid rock, with a thin skin stretched over it.

I had *dreamed* heroism, like everybody, but I had had no practice and I didn't know how to begin. I couldn't bear to begin with starving. I had already come near to that once or twice in my life and got no real enjoyment out of remembering about it.

Grief can take care of itself; but to get the full value of a joy you must have somebody to divide it with.

Titles of honor and dignity once acquired in a democracy, even by accident and properly usable for only forty-eight hours, are as permanent here as eternity is in heaven.

War talk by men who have been in a war is always interesting; whereas moon talk by a poet who has not been in the moon is likely to be dull.

Everything human is pathetic. The secret source of humor itself is not joy but sorrow. There is no humor in heaven.

Africa has been coolly divided up and portioned out among the gang as if they had bought it and paid for it.

There is no family in America without a clock, and consequently there is no fair pretext for the usual Sunday medley of dreadful sounds that issues from our steeples.

I could have become a soldier myself if I had waited. I had got part of it learned; I knew more about retreating than the man that invented retreating.

He poured for us a beverage which he called *"Slumgullion,"* and it is hard to think he was not inspired when he named it. It really pretended to be tea, but there was too much dish-rag, and sand, and old bacon-rind in it to deceive the intelligent traveler.

French morality is not of that strait-laced description which is shocked at trifles.

A long sea-voyage not only brings out all the mean traits one has, and exaggerates them, but raises up others which he never suspected he possessed, and even creates new ones.

Nothing so needs reforming as other people's habits.

Nearly all black and brown skins are beautiful, but a beautiful white skin is rare.

Thunder is good, thunder is impressive; but it is lightning that does the work.

Good breeding consists in concealing how much we think of ourselves and how little we think of the other person.

A sin takes on new and real terrors when there seems a chance that it is going to be found out.

The best swordsman in the world doesn't need to fear the second best swordsman in the world; no, the person for him to be afraid of is some ignorant antagonist who has never had a sword in his hand before; he doesn't do the thing he ought to do, and so the expert isn't prepared for him; he does the thing he ought not to do; and often it catches the expert out and ends him on the spot.

The adoption of cremation would relieve us of a muck of threadbare burial-witticisms; but, on the other hand, it would resurrect a lot of mildewed old cremation-jokes that have had a rest for two thousand years.

His face was as blank as a target after a militia shooting-match.

By and by you sober down, and then you perceive that you have been drunk on the smell of somebody else's cork.

Don't part with your illusions. When they are gone you may still exist but you have ceased to live.

A home without a cat — and a well-fed, well-petted and properly revered cat — may be a perfect home, perhaps, but how can it prove title?

If the desire to kill and the opportunity to kill came always together, who would escape hanging?

There are two times in a man's life when he should not speculate: when he can't afford it, and when he can.

It can be no sufficient compensation to a corpse to know that the dynamite that laid him out was not of as good a quality as it had been supposed to be.

Figures often beguile me, particularly when I have the arranging of them myself; in which case the remark attributed to Disraeli would often apply with justice and force: "There are three kinds of lies: lies, damned lies and statistics."

A soap bubble is the most beautiful thing, and the most exquisite, in nature.

I have traveled more than anyone else, and I have noticed that even the angels speak English with an accent.

When whole races and peoples conspire to propagate gigantic mute lies in the interest of tyrannies and shams, why should we care anything about the trifling lies told by individuals?

In the first place God made idiots. This was for practice. Then He made School Boards.

When your watch gets out of order you have a choice of two things to do: throw it in the fire, or take it to the watch-tinker. The former is the quickest.

April 1. This is the day upon which we are reminded of what we are on the other three hundred and sixty-four.

There warn't anybody at the church, except maybe a hog or two, for there warn't any lock on the door, and hogs like a puncheon floor in summer-time because it's cool. If you notice, most folks don't go to church only when they've got to; but a hog is different.

The very ink with which all history is written is merely fluid prejudice.

Repetition is a mighty power in the domain of humor. If frequently used, nearly any precisely worded and unchanging formula will eventually compel laughter if it be gravely and earnestly repeated, at intervals, five or six times.

Thousands of geniuses live and die undiscovered — either by themselves or by others.

It's better to keep your mouth shut and appear stupid than to open it and remove all doubt.

When red-headed people are above a certain social grade their hair is auburn.

I knew that in Biblical times if a man committed a sin the extermination of the whole surrounding nation — cattle and all — was likely to happen. I knew that Providence was not particular about the rest, so that He got somebody connected with the one He was after.

Whenever the literary German dives into a sentence, that is the last you are going to see of him till he emerges on the other side of his Atlantic with his verb in his mouth.

He didn't utter a word, but he exuded mute blasphemy from every pore.

It takes your enemy and your friend, working together, to hurt you to the heart: the one to slander you and the other to get the news to you.

The first time I ever saw St. Louis I could have bought it for six million dollars, and it was the mistake of my life that I did not do it.

To succeed in the other trades, capacity must be shown; in the law, concealment of it will do.

We have a criminal jury system which is superior to any in the world and its efficiency is only marred by the difficulty of finding twelve men every day who don't know anything and can't read.

The true Southern watermelon is a boon apart, and not to be mentioned with commoner things. It is chief of this world's luxuries, king by the grace of God over all the fruits of the earth. When one has tasted it, he knows what the angels eat. It was not a Southern watermelon that Eve took; we know it because she repented.

Truth is good manners; manners are a fiction.

Man is a museum of diseases, a home of impurities; he comes today and is gone tomorrow; he begins as dirt and departs as stench.

Let us endeavor so to live that when we come to die even the undertaker will be sorry.

If she had had a cork she would have been a comfort. But you can't cork that kind; they would die. Her clack was going all day, and you would think something would surely happen to her works, by and by; but no, they never got out of order; and she never had to slack up for words.

He had had much experience of physicians, and said, "The only way to keep your health is to eat what you don't want, drink what you don't like, and do what you'd druther not."

He was good-natured, obliging and immensely ignorant, and was endowed with a stupidity which by the least little stretch would go around the globe four times and tie.

[Billy Nye] was the baldest human being I ever saw. His whole skull was brilliantly shining. It was like a dome with the sun flashing upon it. He had hardly even a fringe of hair. Once somebody admitted astonishment at his extraordinary baldness. "Oh," he said, "it is nothing: you ought to see my brother."

One day he fell overboard from a ferry boat and when he came up a woman's voice broke high over the tumult of frightened and anxious exclamations and said, "You shameless thing! And ladies present! Go down and come up the other way."

I had ridden around the big island (Hawaii) on horseback and had brought back so many saddle boils that if there had been a duty on them it would have bankrupted me to pay it.

The principal difference between a cat and a lie is that a cat has only nine lives.

When a person cannot deceive himself the chances are against his being able to deceive other people.

We haven't all had the good fortune to be ladies; we haven't all been generals, or poets, or statesmen; but when the toast works down to the babies, we stand on common ground.

I am no lazier now than I was forty years ago, but that is because I reached the limit forty years ago. You can't go beyond possibility.

Nothing is so ignorant as a man's left hand, except a lady's watch.

He is useless on top of the ground; he ought to be under it, inspiring the cabbages.

The habits of all peoples are determined by their circumstances. The Bermudians lean upon barrels because of the scarcity of lamp-posts.

It is a pity that we cannot escape from life when we are young.

You can't depend on your eyes when your imagination is out of focus.

He died two years ago of over-cerebration. He was a poor sort of a creature and by nature and training a fraud. As a liar he was well enough and had some success but no distinction.

It takes some little time to accept and realize the fact that while you have been growing old, your friends have not been standing still.

Mules and donkeys and camels have appetites that anything will relieve temporarily, but nothing satisfy.

There is here and there an American who will say he can remember rising from a European *table d'hôte* perfectly satisfied; but we must not overlook the fact that there is also here and there an American who will lie.

Against a diseased imagination demonstration goes for nothing.

Habit is habit, and not to be flung out of the window by any man, but coaxed downstairs a step at a time.

One must stand on his head to get the best effect in a fine sunset, and set a landscape in a bold, strong framework that is very close at hand, to bring out all its beauty.

We despise all reverences and all the objects of reverence which are outside the pale of our own list of sacred things. And yet, with strange inconsistency, we are shocked when other people despise and defile the things which are holy to us.

It isn't what sum you get, it's how much you can buy with it, that's the important thing; and it's that that tells whether your wages are high in fact or only high in name.

He could foretell wars and famines, though that was not so hard, for there was always a war and generally a famine somewhere.

I thoroughly disapprove of duels. I consider them unwise and I know they are dangerous. Also, sinful. If a man should challenge me now I would go to that man and take him kindly and forgivingly by the hand and lead him to a quiet retired spot and *kill* him.

In any community, big or little, there is always a fair proportion of people who are not malicious or unkind by nature, and who never do unkind things except when they are overmastered by fear, or when their self-interest is in danger.

There are several good protections against temptation: but the surest is cowardice.

We can secure other people's approval, if we do right and try hard; but our own is worth a hundred of it, and no way has been found of securing that.

I know the taste of the watermelon which has been honestly come by, and I know the taste of the watermelon which has been acquired by art. Both taste good, but the experienced know which tastes best.

To spell correctly is a talent, not an acquirement.There is some dignity about an acquirement, because it is a product of your own labor. It is wages earned, whereas to be able to do a thing merely by the grace of God and not by your own effort transfers the distinction to our heavenly home — where possibly it is a matter of pride and satisfaction but it leaves you naked and bankrupt.

We have not the reverent feeling for the rainbow that the savage has, because we know how it is made. We have lost as much as we gained by prying into that matter.

It was ever thus, all through my life: whenever I have diverged from custom and principle and uttered a truth, the rule has been that the hearer hadn't strength of mind enough to believe it.

Scotch whisky to a Scotchman is as innocent as milk is to the rest of the human race.

There are people who strictly deprive themselves of each and every eatable, drinkable and smokable which has in any way acquired a shady reputation. They pay this price for health. And health is all they get. How strange it is! It is like paying out your whole fortune for a cow that has gone dry!

A crime persevered in a thousand centuries ceases to be a crime, and becomes a virtue.

From the beginning of my sojourn in this world there was a persistent vacancy in me where the industry ought to be. ("Ought to was" is better, perhaps, though the most of the authorities differ as to this.)

It is sound judgment to put on a bold face and play your hand for a hundred times what it is worth; forty-nine times out of fifty nobody dares to "call," and you roll in the chips.

In Paris they just simply opened their eyes and stared when we spoke to them in French! We never did succeed in making those idiots understand their own language.

Training is everything. The peach was once a bitter almond; cauliflower is nothing but cabbage with a college education.

Behold the fool saith, "Put not all thine eggs in the one basket" — which is but a manner of saying, "Scatter your money and your attention"; but the wise man saith, "Put all your eggs in the one basket and — *watch that basket*."

It is not worth while to strain one's self to tell the truth to people who habitually discount everything you tell them, whether it is true or isn't.

I have always felt friendly toward Satan. Of course that is ancestral; it must be in the blood, for I could not have originated it.

One mustn't criticise other people on grounds where he can't stand perpendicular himself.

The rich don't care for anybody but themselves; it's only the poor that have feeling for the poor, and help them.

In true beauty, more depends upon right location and judicious distribution of feature than upon multiplicity of them. So also as regards color. The very combination of colors which in a volcanic irruption would add beauty to a landscape might detach it from a girl.

You aim for the palace and get drowned in the sewer.

Whenever we have a strong and persistent and ineradicable instinct we may be sure that it is not original with us but inherited —inherited from away back and hardened and perfected by the petrifying influence of time.

I have noticed my conscience for many years, and I know it is more trouble and bother to me than anything else I started with.

Thanksgiving Day. Let all give humble, hearty, and sincere thanks, now, but the turkeys. In the island of Fiji they do not use turkeys; they use plumbers. It does not become you and me to sneer at Fiji.

Whether he was good, bad or indifferent, he was the Lord's, and nothing that was the Lord's was a thing to be neglected.

When a teacher calls a boy by his entire name it means trouble.

Trial by jury is the palladium of our liberties. I do not know what a palladium is, but it is a good thing, no doubt, at any rate.

I thought tamarinds were made to eat, but that was probably not the idea. I ate several, and it seemed to me that they were rather sour that year. They pursed up my lips, till they resembled the stem-end of a tomato, and I had to take my sustenance through a quill for twenty-four hours.

I never resist a temptation to plunder a stranger's premises without feeling insufferably vain about it.

Often it does seem such a pity that Noah and his party did not miss the boat.

Work consists of whatever a body is *obliged* to do, and Play consists of whatever a body is not obliged to do.

One of the pleasantest and most invigorating exercises one can contrive is to run and jump across the Humboldt river till he is overheated, and then drink it dry.

One frequently only finds out how really beautiful a really beautiful woman is after considerable acquaintance with her; and the rule applies to Niagara Falls, to majestic mountains, and to mosques — especially to mosques.

Truth *is* stranger than Fiction, but it is because Fiction is obliged to stick to possibilities; Truth isn't.

Carlyle said "a lie cannot live." It shows that he did not know how to tell them.

He said that man's heart was the only bad heart in the animal kingdom; that man was the only animal capable of feeling malice, envy, vindictiveness, revengefulness, hatred, selfishness, the only animal that loved drunkenness, almost the only animal that could endure personal uncleanliness and a filthy habitation, the sole animal in whom was fully developed the base instinct called *patriotism,* the sole animal that robs, persecutes, oppresses and kills members of his own immediate tribe, the sole animal that steals and enslaves the members of *any* tribe.

History is full of this old Church of the Holy Sepulcher — full of blood that was shed because of the respect and the veneration in which men held the last resting-place of the meek and lowly, the mild and gentle Prince of Peace!

Neapolitans always ask four times as much money as they intend to take, but if you give them what they first demand, they feel ashamed of themselves for aiming so low, and immediately ask more.

Why do you sit there looking like an envelope without any address on it and see me going mad before your face with suspense?

When I was younger I could remember anything, whether it had happened or not; but my faculties are decaying now and soon I shall be so I cannot remember any but the things that never happened. It is sad to go to pieces like this but we all have to do it.

The autocrat of Russia possesses more power than any other man in the earth; but he cannot stop a sneeze.

All war must be just . . . the killing of strangers against whom you feel no personal animosity; strangers whom, in other circumstances, you would help if you found them in trouble, and who would help you if you needed it.

There comes a time in every rightly-constructed boy's life when he has a raging desire to go somewhere and dig for hidden treasure.

We must put up with our clothes as they are — they have their reason for existing. They are on us to expose us — to advertise what we wear them to conceal. They are a sign; a sign of insincerity; a sign of suppressed vanity; a pretense that we desire gorgeous colors and the graces of harmony and form; and we put them on to propagate that lie and back it up.

The timid man yearns for full value, and asks a tenth; the bold man strikes for double value, and compromises at par.

My friends and acquaintances looked ashamed and the house, as a body, looked as if it had taken an emetic.

Knowledge was not good for the common people, and could make them discontented with the lot which God had appointed for them, and God would not endure discontentment with His plans.

No brute ever does a cruel thing — that is the monopoly of those with the moral sense. When a brute inflicts pain he does it innocently; it is not wrong; for him there is no such thing as wrong. And he does not inflict pain for the pleasure of inflicting it — only man does that.

The man who is born stingy can be taught to give liberally — with his hands; but not with his heart.

That is the main charm of heaven—there's all kinds here—which wouldn't be the case if you let the preachers tell it. Anybody can find the sort he prefers, here, and he just lets the others alone, and they let him alone. When the Deity builds a heaven, it is built right, and on a liberal plan.

The highest perfection of politeness is only a beautiful edifice, built, from the base to the dome, of graceful and gilded forms of charitable and unselfish lying.

There is an old-time toast which is golden for its beauty: "When you ascend the hill of prosperity may you not meet a friend."

It is by the goodness of God that in our country we have those three unspeakably precious things: freedom of speech, freedom of conscience, and the prudence never to practice either of them.

He had no principles and was delightful company.

My mother had a great deal of trouble with me but I think she enjoyed it.

There is nothing in the world like a persuasive speech to fuddle the mental apparatus and upset the convictions and debauch the emotions of an audience not practiced in the tricks and delusions of oratory.

Unlimited power *is* the ideal thing when it is in safe hands. The despotism of heaven is the one absolutely perfect government. Do I seem to be preaching? It is out of my line: I only do it because the rest of the clergy seem to be on vacation.

What are the proper proportions of a maxim? A minimum of sound to a maximum of sense.

The *spirit* of wrath — not the words — is the sin; and the spirit of wrath is cursing. We begin to swear before we can talk.

Let me make the superstitions of a nation and I care not who makes its laws or its songs either.

Even the clearest and most perfect circumstantial evidence is likely to be at fault, *after* all, and therefore ought to be received with great caution. Take the case of any pencil, sharpened by any woman: if you have witnesses, you will find she did it with a knife; but if you take simply the aspect of the pencil, you will say she did it with her teeth.

An ecstasy is a thing that will not go into words; it feels like music, and one cannot tell about music so that another person can get the feeling of it.

Territorial Governors . . . are nothing but politicians who go out to the outskirts of countries and suffer the privations there in order to build up stakes and come back as United States Senators.

Why is it that we rejoice at a birth and grieve at a funeral? It is because we are not the person involved.

[The ass] said that when it took a whole basketful of sesquipedalian adjectives to whoop up a thing of beauty, it was time for suspicion.

All say, "How hard it is that we have to die" — a strange complaint to come from the mouths of people who have had to live.

Let us be thankful for the fools. But for them the rest of us could not succeed.

The fountains of her great deep were broken up, and she rained the nine parts of speech forty days and forty nights, metaphorically speaking, and buried us under a desolating deluge of trivial gossip that left not a crag or pinnacle of rejoinder projecting above the tossing waste of dislocated grammar and decomposed pronunciation!

Few things are harder to put up with than the annoyance of a good example.

Let us not be too particular. It is better to have old second-hand diamonds than none at all.

It could probably be shown by facts and figures that there is no distinctly native American criminal class except Congress.

Truth is the most valuable thing we have. Let us economize it.

In these latter days it seems hard to realize that there was ever a time when the robbing of our government was a novelty.

Few slanders can stand the wear of silence.

Each boy has one or two sensitive spots and if you can find out where they are located you have only to touch them and you can scorch him as with fire.

Forget and forgive. This is not difficult, when properly understood. It means that you are to forget inconvenient duties, and forgive yourself for forgetting. In time, by rigid practice and stern determination, it comes easy.

We adore titles and heredities in our hearts and ridicule them with our mouths. This is our democratic privilege.

Many a notorious coward, many a chicken-hearted poltroon, coarse, brutal, degraded, has made his dying speech without a quaver in his voice and been swung into eternity with what looked like the calmest fortitude.

Custom is a petrifaction; nothing but dynamite can dislodge it for a century.

He imagined that he was in love with her, whereas I think she did the imagining for him.

But in my age, as in my youth, night brings me many a deep remorse. I realize that from the cradle up I have been like the rest of the race — never quite sane in the night.

When teeth became touched with decay or were otherwise ailing, the doctor knew of but one thing to do — he fetched his tongs and dragged them out. If the jaw remained, it was not his fault.

Each person is born to one possession which outvalues all his others — his last breath.

Oriental scenes look best in steel engravings. I cannot be imposed upon any more by that picture of the Queen of Sheba visiting Solomon. I shall say to myself, You look fine, madam, but your feet are not clean, and you smell like a camel.

One gets large impressions in boyhood, sometimes, which he has to fight against all his life.

Every man is a suffering-machine and a happiness-machine combined. The two functions work together harmoniously, with a fine and delicate precision, on the give-and-take principle. For every happiness turned out in the one department the other stands ready to modify it with a sorrow or a pain — maybe a dozen.

I thought I was lazy, but I am a steam engine compared to a Constantinople dog.

I have criticised absent people so often, and then discovered, to my humiliation, that I was talking with their relatives, that I have grown superstitious about that sort of thing and dropped it.

Any mummery will cure if the patient's faith is strong in it.

The proverb says that Providence protects children and idiots. This is really true. I know it because I have tested it.

If you pick up a starving dog and make him prosperous, he will not bite you. This is the principal difference between a dog and a man.

They spell it Vinci and pronounce it Vinchy; foreigners always spell better than they pronounce.

I was gratified to be able to answer promptly, and I did. I said I didn't know.

The government of my country snubs honest simplicity, but fondles artistic villainy, and I think I might have developed into a very capable pickpocket if I had remained in the public service a year or two.

Man will do many things to get himself loved, he will do all things to get himself envied.

None of us can ever have as many virtues as the fountain pen, or half its cussedness; but we can try.

We were little Christian children and had early been taught the value of forbidden fruit.

Beautiful credit! The foundation of modern society. Who shall say that this is not the golden age of mutual trust, of unlimited reliance upon human promises?

Sage-brush is very fair fuel, but as a vegetable it is a distinguished failure. Nothing can abide the taste of it but the jackass and his illegitimate child, the mule.

No country can be well governed unless its citizens as a body keep religiously before their minds that they are the guardians of the law, and that the law officers are only the machinery for its execution, nothing more.

When he found that I had come to sell a book and not to buy one, his temperature fell sixty degrees and the old-gold-intrenchments in the roof of my mouth contracted three-quarters of an inch and my teeth fell out.

I have witnessed and greatly enjoyed the first act of everything which Wagner created, but the effect on me has always been so powerful that one act was quite sufficient; whenever I have witnessed two acts I have gone away physically exhausted; and whenever I have ventured an entire opera the result has been the next thing to suicide.

After all these years, I see that I was mistaken about Eve in the beginning; it is better to live outside the Garden with her than inside it without her.

A man pretty much always refuses another man's first offer, no matter what it is.

Consider well the proportion of things. It is better to be a young June-bug than an old bird of paradise.

Can it be possible that the painters make John the Baptist a Spaniard in Madrid and an Irishman in Dublin?

There are times when one would like to hang the whole human race and finish the farce.

Occasionally, merely for the pleasure of being cruel, we put unoffending Frenchmen on the rack with questions framed in the incomprehensible jargon of their native language, and while they writhed, we impaled them, we peppered them, we sacrificed them, with their own vile verbs and participles.

There are people who think that honesty is always the best policy. This is a superstition; there are times when the appearance of it is worth six of it.

Uncle Abner said that the person that had took a bull by the tail once had learnt sixty or seventy times as much as a person that hadn't, and said a person that started in to carry a cat home by the tail was gitting knowledge that was always going to be useful to him, and warn't ever going to grow dim or doubtful.

The man with a new idea is a Crank, until the idea succeeds.

She was not quite what you would call refined, she was not quite what you would call unrefined. She was the kind of person that keeps a parrot.

The reason novelists nearly always fail in depicting women when they make them act, is that they let them do what they have observed some woman has done at some time or another. And that is where they make a mistake; for a woman will never do again what has been done before.

When we inherit property, it does not occur to us to throw it away, even when we do not want it.

No people in the world ever did achieve their freedom by goody-goody talk and moral suasion: it being immutable law that all revolutions that will succeed must *begin* in blood, whatever may answer afterward.

There are those who scoff at the schoolboy, calling him frivolous and shallow. Yet it was the schoolboy who said, "Faith is believing what you know ain't so."

In India "cold weather" is merely a conventional phrase and has come into use through the necessity of having some way to distinguish between weather which will melt a brass door-knob and weather which will only make it mushy.

It is easy to find fault, if one has that disposition. There was once a man who, not being able to find any other fault with his coal, complained that there were too many prehistoric toads in it.

Human pride is not worth while; there is always something lying in wait to take the wind out of it.

Every one is a moon, and has a dark side which he never shows to anybody.

She calculated his capacity as she would a jug's, and filled him up every day with quack cure-alls.

The holy passion of Friendship is of so sweet and steady and loyal and enduring a nature that it will last through a whole lifetime, if not asked to lend money.

There is no character, howsoever good and fine, but it can be destroyed by ridicule, howsoever poor and witless. Observe the ass, for instance: his character is about perfect, he is the choicest spirit among all the humbler animals, yet see what ridicule has brought him to. Instead of feeling complimented when we are called an ass, we are left in doubt.

Words realize nothing, verify nothing to you, unless you have suffered in your own person the thing which the words try to describe.

There isn't a Parallel of Latitude but thinks it would have been the Equator if it had had its rights.

Noise proves nothing. Often a hen who has merely laid an egg cackles as if she has laid an asteroid.

October. This is one of the peculiarly dangerous months to speculate in stocks in. The others are July, January, September, April, November, May, March, June, December, August, and February.

July 4. Statistics show that we lose more fools on this day than on all the other days of the year put together. This proves, by the number left in stock, that one Fourth of July per year is inadequate, the country has grown so.

The church is always trying to get other people to reform; it might not be a bad idea to reform itself a little, by way of example.

Reverence for one's own sacred things — parents, religion, flag, laws, and respect for one's own beliefs — these are feelings which we cannot even help. They come natural to us; they are involuntary, like breathing. There is no personal merit in breathing.

Few of us can stand prosperity. Another man's, I mean.

Punjabi proverb. The altar-cloth of one aeon is the doormat of the next.

The best way to get a sure thing on a fact is to go and examine it for yourself, and not take anybody's say-so.

Always do right. This will gratify some people, and astonish the rest.

The calm confidence of a Christian with four aces.

In Marseilles they make half the fancy toilet soap we consume in America, but the Marseillaise only have a vague theoretical idea of its use, which they have obtained from books of travel.

Human nature is *very* much the same all over the world; and it is *so* like my dear native home to see a Venetian lady go into a store and buy ten cents' worth of blue ribbon and have it sent home in a scow. Ah, it is these little touches of nature that move one to tears in these far-off foreign lands.

One can gorge on sights to repletion as well as sweetmeats.

If you should rear a duck in the heart of the Sahara, no doubt it would swim if you brought it to the Nile.

Wrinkles should merely indicate where the smiles have been.

It is popular to admire the Arno. It is a great historical creek with four feet in the channel and some scows floating around. It would be a plausible river if they would pump some water into it.

The gentle reader will never, never know what a consummate ass he can become until he goes abroad.

Simple rules for saving money. To save half: When you are fired by an eager impulse to contribute to a charity, wait, and count forty. To save three-quarters, count sixty. To save it all, count sixty-five.

Many a small thing has been made large by the right kind of advertising.

We should be careful to get out of an experience only the wisdom that is in it — and stay there, lest we be like the cat that sits down on a hot stove-lid. She will never sit down on a hot stove-lid again — and that is well; but also she will never sit down on a cold one any more.

When you are expecting the worst, you get something that is not so bad, after all.

His air was so natural and so simple that one was always catching himself accepting his stately sentences as meaning something, when they really meant nothing in the world.

She is a shining drop of quicksilver which you put your finger on and it isn't there.

The true desperado is gifted with splendid courage, and yet he will take the most infamous advantage of his enemy; armed and free, he will stand up before a host and fight until he is shot all to pieces, and yet when he is under the gallows and helpless he will cry and plead like a child.

India has two million gods, and worships them all. In religion all other countries are paupers; India is the only millionaire.

When I reflect upon the number of disagreeable people who I know have gone to a better world, I am moved to lead a different life.

Sir Walter [Scott] had so large a hand in making southern character, as it existed before the war, that he is in great measure responsible for the war.

Its name is Public Opinion. It is held in reverence. It settles everything. Some think it is the voice of God.

There is a great difference between feeding parties to wild beasts and stirring up their finer feelings in an inquisition. One is the system of degraded barbarians, the other of enlightened civilized people.

There are three kinds of people — Commonplace Men, Remarkable Men, and Lunatics.

The *can-can*. The idea of it is to dance as wildly, as noisily, as furiously as you can; expose yourself as much as possible if you are a woman; and kick as high as you can, no matter which sex you belong to.

Mastery of the art and spirit of the Germanic language . . . enables a man to travel all day in one sentence without changing cars.

If the man doesn't believe as we do, we say he is a crank, and that settles it. I mean it does nowadays, because we can't burn him.

If there is one thing that will make a man peculiarly and insufferably self-conceited, it is to have his stomach behave itself, the first day at sea, when nearly all his comrades are seasick.

Alas! those good old days are gone, when a murderer could wipe the stain from his name and soothe his trouble to sleep simply by getting out his blocks and mortar and building an addition to a church.

Gold in its native state is but dull, unornamental stuff, and . . . only lowborn metals excite the admiration of the ignorant with an ostentatious glitter. However, like the rest of the world, I still go on underrating men of gold and glorifying men of mica.

He was as shy as a newspaper is when referring to its own merits.

I wish there was something in that miserable spiritualism, so we could send them word.

Schoolboy days are no happier than the days of after life, but we look back upon them regretfully because we have forgotten our punishments at school, and how we grieved when our marbles were lost and our kites destroyed—because we have forgotten all the sorrows and privations of that canonized epoch and remember only its orchard robberies, its wooden sword pageants, and its fishing holidays.

It is more trouble to make a maxim than it is to do right.

The man who is ostentatious of his modesty is twin to the statue that wears a fig-leaf.

When a person of mature age perpetrates a practical joke it is fair evidence, I think, that he is weak in the head and hasn't enough heart to signify.

To be the *first* — that is the idea. To do something, say something, see something, before *anybody* else — these are the things that confer a pleasure compared with which other pleasures are tame and commonplace, other ecstasies cheap and trivial.

The stars ain't so close together as they look to be.

We ought never to do wrong when people are looking.

When one writes a novel about grown people, he knows exactly where to stop — that is, with a marriage; but when he writes of juveniles, he must stop where best he can.

Death, the only immortal who treats us all alike, whose pity and whose peace and whose refuge are for all — the soiled and the pure, the rich and the poor, the loved and the unloved.

The reports of my death are greatly exaggerated.